Making a Milking Stool

John Boakes

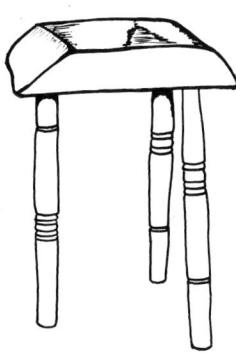

Smith
Settle

First published in 2001 by
Smith Settle Ltd
Ilkley Road
Otley
West Yorkshire
LS21 3JP

© John Boakes 2001

ISBN 1 85825 119 2

British Library Cataloguing-in-Publication data:
A catalogue record for this book is available from the British Library.

Set in Monotype Plantin

Designed, printed and bound by
SMITH SETTLE
Ilkley Road, Otley, West Yorkshire LS21 3JP

Introduction

Bodging has been practised in the ancient beech woods of England and Scotland for centuries. The skilled and sensitive *bodger* was a man who worked in the woods using freshly cut unseasoned wood to produce all manner of pieces of household ware. These pieces, called *treen*, included bowls, platters, spoons, containers for spices etc, and, of course, chairs and the ubiquitous three-legged milking stool.

The tools the bodger used were few and commonplace, including an axe and a cross-cut saw for felling the timber, though in recent years these have commonly been replaced by the modern-day chainsaw. A *beetle* and *froe* were used for cleaving the sawn pieces, then a hatchet and *drawshave* were needed to roughly shape the lengths of wood; finally a pole lathe and various turning chisels finished off the work.

In recent times there have been very few such people left to continue this ancient craft, although today, with growing interest in the environment and recycling, there are once again more people attracted to the art of bodging.

Before the last war, the bodgers' work was centred mainly in the large traditional coppiced woods. These woods would have supported many different craftsmen producing such diverse items as treen, chair legs, saddle trees, clogs and charcoal to name a few. The greatest number of bodgers in the country were centred around the great native woodlands of the Chiltern Hills near High Wycombe, Stokenchurch and Penn. There were also smaller groups working in the large woods on the North and South Downs. Here the native beech (*Fagus sylvatica*) grew in large numbers and provided the raw material for the bodgers' work.

The bodgers' continual need for the correct-sized wood with which to work was achieved by a selection system called *coppicing*, the word coming from the French *couper*, meaning to cut. This was a process whereby trees of a certain size and thickness were cut down to provide enough material for the bodgers to use each season. The smaller trees were left to grow and mature to the correct size, when they too would be felled. By this managed method, with cutting every seven years or so, the wood continually provided the material needed by the many different craftsmen.

These craftsmen spent the six months of the summer living in the woods in a flimsy, makeshift shelter called a *bodgers' hovel*. This meant that they could live within the confines of the woods as they worked. In this way they did not incur carting costs in carrying the timber for any great distances to the workshops; also, by living in the woods, any waste pieces of timber not used in their work was used as fuel for their cooking fires.

Most of the bodgers' work was made mainly from beech, but occasionally they also used elm and ash. These three varieties were popular because they all could be carved easily on the pole lathe. Many centuries ago, some bodgers would make the odd complete chair, allowing it to season for a short while before selling it in the nearest village. But by the late nineteenth century, these craftsmen were being asked to make whole chairs or sometimes parts of chairs for a local furniture-maker or in some cases a larger factory. The bodgers found it was much quicker and easier to just supply these workshops with only chair legs. Soon other bodgers started to see the benefits of this idea, and also started to make chair legs for the factories. This trade gave the majority of bodgers a good living for many years.

When these legs were finished, they would be stacked in open squares of four to allow the air to flow through them and so season them, before they were finally carted off to the factories to be sold. Using a pole lathe, a good bodger could produce around 800 finished chair legs in a day, which would average out at about one chair leg every four or five minutes. But eventually, when machines became more refined, the factories started to produce their own chair legs. In time, as these factory-made chairs became cheaper and more popular, the main trade for bodgers finally ceased. The decline of bodging continued, so much so that, until the last ten years or so, it was very hard to find a working bodger anywhere in the country at all.

When bodgers were working in the woods, they usually worked in pairs as a team. After they had both felled the timber, one would start preparing and chopping the wood into two foot (60cm) lengths called *billets*. Any thicker-sized timber was cleft with the beetle and froe into several pieces before being cut into roughly the correct size and shape for these billets. These would then be trimmed and shaped on a wooden *horse* with a drawshave, before finally being passed to the second bodger, who turned the billet into a finished chair leg on the pole lathe. With the power source provided by a springy tree, the pole lathe was a very cheap and mobile instrument to use, and in the hands of an expert it was a very precise one, too. There was a knack to using this lathe, for when the treadle was depressed, the piece of wood to be *turned* or shaped was rotated towards the user; and when the treadle was released, it started to rotate away from him. All the turning was done on the down stroke. The pole lathe is probably the oldest form of turning device, and when used by an expert it is able to produce work of the highest quality.

As the bodgers worked in the woods, they utilised any pieces of decent-sized wood that could not be turned in to chair legs by putting them aside to be made into tent pegs. These tent pegs were one of the many other things that bodgers produced. The pegs were very strong because, being made of cleft wood, the grain of the timber was split and not broken, thus giving a good, strong tent peg that could be used time and time again. Modern-day tent pegs are now mostly made from metal, but the few remaining wooden ones still made today are not as good as the old cleft type made by the bodger, because modern-day machinery cuts across the grain of the wood and the resultant peg has very little natural strength.

In the 1920s the once-widespread practice of chair making had centred itself around the Chiltern area. There, bodgers typically made the so-called Windsor chair. (In fact, there were many variations on the Windsor chair made throughout England and Scotland.) This common design was originally called the Windsor chair because George III placed an order for a set for Windsor Castle, the king stipulating that these chairs were to be made along the traditional country design as seen all over the land.

Mike Pratt is lucky enough to be able to combine his work for the North York Moors National Park Authority, where he is an information officer, with his love of the countryside and woodland crafts. Bodging is one of his particular loves since he learnt it from one of the best bodgers in the country over ten years ago in the Forest of Dean. In the latter part of this book, Mike shows us all the different steps in the making of the once-common milking stool.

Bibliography

James Arnold, *The Shell Book of Country Crafts* (1968).
Herbert Edlin, *Woodland Craft of Britain* (1949 & 1973).
H E Fitzrandolph & M D Hay, *The Rural Crafts of England and Wales* (1926 & 1977).
J E Manners, *Country Crafts Today* (1974).

Acknowledgements

The author would like to thank the following for permission to reproduce photographs: Mr H Bastin, pp8, 10-11; David and Charles Publishers, pp8-11; M W Inman, p9; the Rural History Centre at Reading University, p46. The author would also like to thank Mike Pratt of the North York Moors National Park Authority for his help in the preparation of this book.

A makeshift bodger's hovel from the 1940s.

An old-time bodger cleaving newly sawn timber into the right-sized billets.

(Left) Using a beetle and froe to cleave the billets. *(Right)* Shaping the billet with a side axe.

A bodger using his horse to prepare a billet for the pole lathe.

Mike Pratt splitting lengths of cut timber to make the two feet (60cm) long billets.

Then they are split again.

Notice how the two pieces have split along the grain. This is important for the strength of the piece being made.

The three stages of turning
the cut timber into billets
are shown here.

The billets waiting to go
on to the next stage.

The billets are hewn in to a rough circular shape with a side axe.

The rough shaping finished.

Mike gives the billets a final shaping on the horse with a drawshave.

The shavings left on the home-made horse show how much work has been necessary.

The billet is centred on the pole lathe.

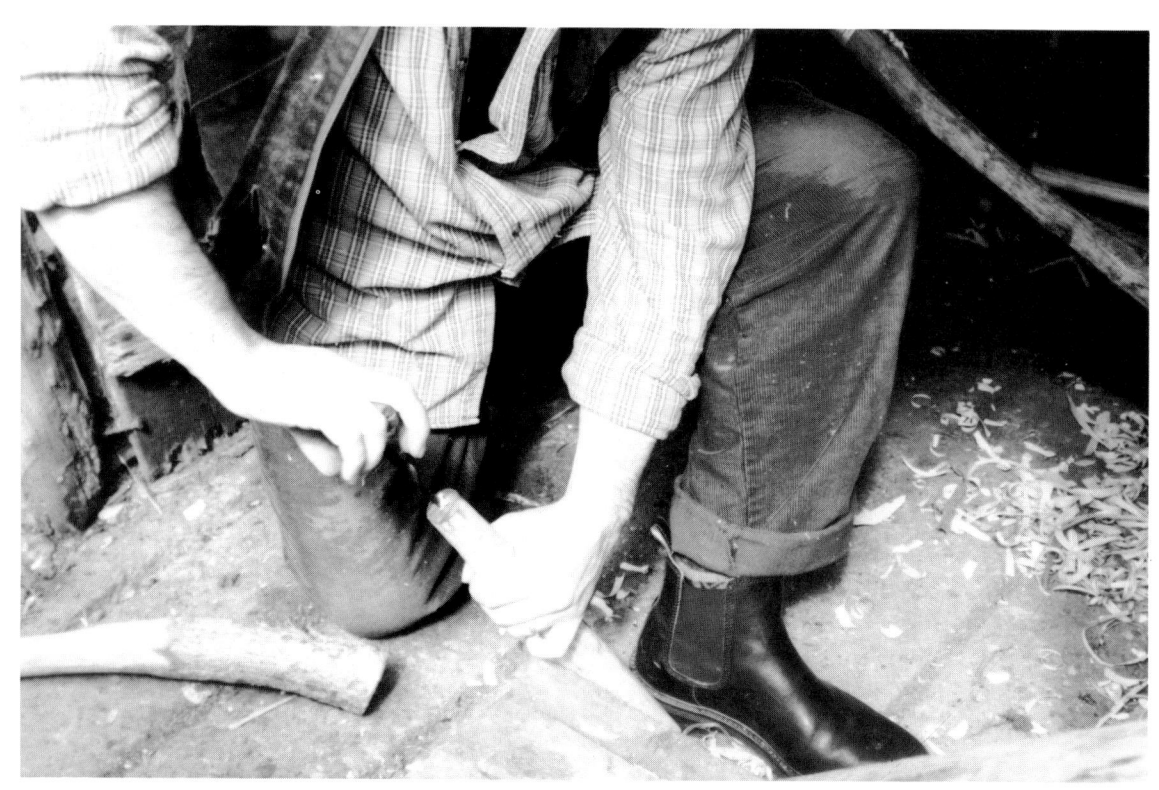

The ends of the billet are marked, then enlarged.

The rotating motion is caused by a string attached to the treadle and a springy length of wood at the other. Two loops are put around the billet.

Then the billet is fixed into position. The hat seen hanging on the end of the pole lathe relates to an old superstition that the user of a pole lathe should always have a hat.

Any slight alterations are made.

The first shaping cuts to make the billet into a perfect cylinder.

The pattern is gradually carved on to the leg.

As the pattern is completed, another superstition says that the bodger must always try to leave a piece of the sap wood on until the last moment of turning. This sap wood is the darker piece on the billet.

When one leg is finished, the position of the pattern is marked off on the other two legs.

Some of the stool legs that Mike has made, waiting for seat tops.

Three holes are drilled in the underside of the seat top with an *auger*.

31

The three finished legs and the top ready for the next stage.

The legs are fitted into
the holes and secured.

Mike shows us the
finished stool.

A selection of the tools needed in bodging.

The complete pole lathe is composed of several different parts.

The two stocks of the pole lathe were the only parts, along with the cord, that the bodger took with him as he went from wood to wood.

The stocks are secured in the bed of the lathe with these two wedges.

The bed of the lathe. In the past, this was usually made up from two halves of newly cleft timber fixed to some legs, also newly felled.

The power source was usually a length of thin springy branch. This is attached by a long cord, which passes round the work to be turned, to the treadle *(pictured)* in the upright position. The treadle itself was secured to the frame by lengths of leather, which allowed the treadle to move up and down as it bent the springy length of wood.

In Mike Pratt's case, the power source is a modern-day equivalent, the elastic bungee.

The simple rest can be secured in several positions in the two guides that are attached to the stock. The different positions allow for different-sized work to be made.

Here the rest is set for the turning of a small treen bowl.

Tent pegs were one of the sidelines that bodgers used to make with any pieces of wood too small to be made into billets.

Some of the other work that Mike has made.

Mr J Davies from Wales making a treen bowl on his pole lathe in 1932.

A pair of Mike's treen spoons. They are made as one and then parted down the middle lengthwise.